MW01256989

Differentiated Reading
for Comprehension

Grade 1

Credits
Content Editor: Hope Spencer
Copy Editor: Karen Seberg
Illustrations: Nick Greenwood, Donald O'Connor

Visit *carsondellosa.com* for correlations to Common Core, state, national, and Canadian provincial standards.

Carson-Dellosa Publishing, LLC
PO Box 35665
Greensboro, NC 27425 USA
carsondellosa.com

ISBN 978-1-4838-0486-6

01-034141151

Table of Contents

Introduction 2
Common Core Alignment Chart 3

Wild Animals
Gentle Giants. 4
Catch Me if You Can! 8
The Huge Hunter 12

Strange and Unexplained
Friend or Foe? 16
It Is Raining Cats and Frogs?. 20

Fascinating Machines
Once Upon a Time 24
Quack, Quack! 28

Amazing Kids
Frozen Delight 32
Talk to the Animals 36
Be Amazing! 40

Amazing People
Warrior Queen 44
Exploring the Arctic. 48

Extreme Places
Digging for Dinosaurs 52
The Amazing Amazon 56
A National Treasure 60

Answer Key 64

Introduction

Providing all students access to high quality, nonfiction text is essential to Common Core State Standards mastery. This book contains exactly what teachers are looking for: high-interest nonfiction passages, each written at three different reading levels, followed by a shared set of text-dependent comprehension questions and a writing prompt to build content knowledge. Both general academic and domain-specific vocabulary words are reinforced at the end of each passage for further comprehension support. The standards listed on each page provide an easy reference tool for lesson planning, and the Common Core Alignment Chart on page 3 allows you to target or remediate specific skills.

The book is comprised of 15 stories that are written at three levels:
- Below level (one dot beside the page number): 1 to 1.5 levels below grade level
- On level (two dots beside the page number): 0 to 0.5 levels below grade level
- Advanced (three dots beside the page number): 1 to 2 levels above grade level

Which students will not enjoy reading about the mighty polar bear or the 11-year-old boy who invented one of our favorite frozen treats or our magnificent first national park? This book will quickly become the go-to resource for differentiated nonfiction reading practice in your classroom!

Common Core Alignment Chart

Common Core State Standards*		Practice Pages
Reading Standards for Informational Text		
Key Ideas and Details	1.RI.1–1.RI.3	7, 11, 15, 23, 31, 35, 39, 47, 51, 55, 63
Craft and Structure	1.RI.4–1.RI.6	19, 27, 43, 51, 59
Integration of Knowledge and Ideas	1.RI.7–1.RI.9	39
Range of Reading and Level of Text Complexity	1.RI.10	4–6, 8–10, 12–14, 16–18, 20–22, 24–26, 28–30, 32–34, 36–38, 40–42, 44–46, 48–50, 52–54, 56–58, 60–62
Reading Standards: Foundational Skills		
Print Concepts	1.RF.1	27
Phonological Awareness	1.RF.2	23
Phonics and Word Recognition	1.RF.3	19, 51
Fluency	1.RF.4	4–6, 8–10, 12–14, 16–18, 20–22, 24–26, 28–30, 32–34, 36–38, 40–42, 44–46, 48–50, 52–54, 56–58, 60–62
Writing Standards		
Text Types and Purposes	1.W.1–1.W.3	11, 15, 19, 23, 27, 35, 39, 43, 47, 51, 55, 59, 63
Production and Distribution of Writing	1.W.5–1.W.6	31
Research to Build and Present Knowledge	1.W.7–1.W.8	7
Language Standards		
Conventions of Standard English	1.L.1–1.L.2	7, 27, 31, 35, 39, 43, 47, 59, 63
Vocabulary Acquisition and Use	1.L.4–1.L.6	4–6, 8–10, 11, 12–14, 16–18, 19, 20–22, 24–26, 28–30, 31, 32–34, 36–38, 40–42, 44–46, 48–50, 52–54, 55, 56–58, 60–62

How to Use This Alignment Chart

The Common Core State Standards for English Language Arts are a shared set of expectations for each grade level in the areas of reading, writing, speaking, listening, and language. They define what students should understand and be able to do. This chart presents the standards that are covered in this book.

Use this chart to plan your instruction, practice, or remediation of a specific standard. To do this, first choose your targeted standard; then, find the pages listed on the chart that correlate to the standard you are teaching. Finally, assign the reading pages and follow-up questions to practice the skill.

Gentle Giants

What if your neck was six feet (1.83 m) long? What if your legs were six feet long? What if both were six feet long? Then, you would be a giraffe. A giraffe is the tallest animal on Earth.

A giraffe is tall. It needs to reach the tops of trees. Giraffes eats leaves. A giraffe uses its tongue to pull leaves off of trees. Its black tongue is 18 inches (45.72 cm) long! A giraffe eats for half of each day. It can eat just a few leaves at a time. The giraffe is so big that it needs a lot of food. It eats about 75 pounds (34.02 kg) of food a day. It chews for a long time!

Adult giraffes are big. Not a lot of animals **hunt** them. But, baby giraffes are small. Some animals try to hunt them. Mothers must **guard** their babies. They keep the babies in groups. One adult watches the group. The mothers leave to eat. If a hunter comes, the adult will kick it away.

Giraffes must bend low to drink. Crocodiles might be in the water. The crocodile might bite the giraffe. The giraffes work as a team. They go to a pond in a group. One giraffe stands guard while the others drink.

Giraffes move in **herds**. You may see one on the African plain and think it is alone. It is not. A giraffe is tall, and it can see very far. It can see over half of a mile (0.8 km) away. The giraffe feels safe as long as it sees its herd. Giraffes make sounds and "talk" to each other while they eat.

hunt: to chase to kill and eat
guard: watch over; protect
herd: group of animals that live together

Gentle Giants

What would you do if your neck was six feet (1.83 m) long? What would you do if your legs were six feet long? What would you do if your neck and your legs were both six feet long? Then, you would be the tallest animal on Earth. You would be a giraffe.

Why is a giraffe so tall? Its height helps it reach the tops of trees. It eats the leaves at the tops of trees. The giraffe has a long black tongue. Its tongue is 18 inches (45.72 cm) long. The tongue helps it pull leaves off of the trees. A giraffe spends half of each day eating. A giraffe can eat just a few leaves at a time. Because it is so big, it eats about 75 pounds (34.02 kg) of food a day. It chews for a long time!

Adult giraffes are big. Other animals do not bother them. But, baby giraffes are small. Animals like lions may try to **hunt** them. Mother giraffes have a way to **guard** their babies. One adult tends a group of babies. The other mothers go off to eat. If a lion comes close, the adult giraffe kicks it away.

When giraffes drink, they bend their heads very low. A crocodile might try to bite them when they bend down. Giraffes work as a team to get water. They go to a pond together. One giraffe stands guard while the others drink.

Giraffes always move in **herds.** If you see one on the African plain, it may look alone. It is not. It can see over half of a mile (0.8 km) away. A giraffe feels safe if it can still see its herd. Giraffes will moo, hiss, and whistle to "talk" to each other as they eat.

hunt: to chase to kill and eat
guard: watch over; protect
herd: group of animals that live together

Gentle Giants

Imagine having a six-foot (1.83 m) long neck! Now, imagine that your legs are six feet long, too. That would make you the tallest animal on Earth. Welcome to the world of the giraffe.

Why is the giraffe so tall? Its long legs and long neck help it eat leaves from the tops of trees. The giraffe uses its 18-inch (45.72 cm) long black tongue to help it pull leaves off trees. This animal giant spends at least half of each day eating. It can eat just a few leaves at a time. Because it is so big, a giraffe eats about 75 pounds (34.02 kg) a day.

Adult giraffes are very big. They do not have a lot of enemies. But, baby giraffes do. Meat-eating animals like lions try to kill the babies. Mother giraffes have a **system** to **guard** their babies. One adult watches over a group of babies. The other mothers go off to eat. If a lion comes close, the adult giraffe kicks it away.

Giraffes bend very low to drink. A crocodile may try to bite them when they drink. Giraffes work as a team to get water. They go to a pond in a group. One giraffe stands guard while the others drink water.

Giraffes always move in **herds**. When you see one on the African plain, it might look alone. It is not. A giraffe is so tall that it can see over half of a mile (0.8 km) away. As long as it can see the rest of its herd, it feels safe. Giraffes will moo, hiss, and whistle to "talk" to each other as they eat.

imagine: form an idea in your mind
system: a set of ideas; an arrangement
guard: watch over; protect
herd: group of animals that live together

 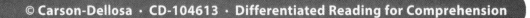

Gentle Giants

Answer the questions.

1. Why does the giraffe spend so much time eating?

    A. It likes to eat strange foods.

    B. It is so big that it needs a lot of food.

    C. It has to find food for its babies.

    D. Its neck is so long.

2. Which of the following is a feature of the giraffe?

    A. 18-inch (45.72 cm) long legs

    B. a red tongue

    C. a six-foot (1.83 m) long tail

    D. six-foot (1.83 m) long legs

3. _____ might attack giraffes when they drink water.

4. A giraffe can eat only a few _____ at a time.

Circle the correct verb for each sentence.

5. An adult giraffe (watch, watched) the group yesterday.

6. Last week, a giraffe (walk, walked) on the African plain.

7. Today, a lion (hunts, hunted) for a giraffe.

8. Giraffes work in groups to protect and help each other. Think of a time when you worked in a group to finish a task. What was the task? Write about your experience working with the group. Write your paragraph on another sheet of paper.

Catch Me if You Can!

Many animals on the African grassland hunt their food. Those that do not want to be caught have to run. The cheetah seems to know this. It is the fastest land animal on Earth. A cheetah can be running fast in just three steps. In fact, a cheetah can run 40 miles (64.37 km) to 70 miles (112.65 km) per hour!

The cheetah is built to run fast. It has long legs. It has hard **pads** on its paws. The paws help it stop. The cheetah also has large **lungs**. Its lungs help it take deep breaths. And, it has dark marks under its eyes. They keep the sun from blinding the cheetah. The cheetah's bones are lightweight too. All of this helps it run fast.

The cheetah is a good hunter. It must guard the food it kills. Large animals, like lions, might take the meat. Then, the cheetah has no food that day. It cannot hunt twice in one day. It runs so fast that it has to rest.

A mother cheetah shows her young how to hunt. She hurts a small animal. Then, she brings it to her cubs. They chase and kill it. The cubs play games too. The games help them run fast. They play games that we know. They play tag, and they wrestle. The cubs will be good hunters when they are about three years old.

After the cubs grow up, the females leave. They go off on their own. They have their own cubs. Brother cheetahs might stay together for life. They work as a team to hunt. They pick a **territory**. That is where they hunt. They protect the land together.

pad: thick cushion on the bottom of an animal's foot
lungs: the organs in the body that allow creatures to breathe; part of the respiratory system
territory: an area an animal or group of animals lives in and defends

Catch Me if You Can!

Many animals on the African grassland hunt their food. Those that do not want to be eaten have to run. The cheetah seems to know this. It is the fastest land animal on Earth. A cheetah can go from standing still to running fast in just three steps. In fact, a cheetah can run 40 miles (64.37 km) to 70 miles (112.65 km) per hour!

The cheetah is built to run fast. It has long legs. It has hard **pads** on its paws. The paws help it stop. The cheetah also has large **lungs**. Its lungs help it take very deep breaths. And, it has dark marks under its eyes. The marks look like black tears. They **reflect** the sun and keep it from blinding the cheetah. Its bones are lightweight too. All of this helps it run fast.

The cheetah is a good hunter. It has to guard the food it kills. Large animals, like lions, might take the meat. Then, the cheetah has no food that day. It cannot hunt twice in one day. It has to rest after running so fast.

A mother cheetah shows her young how to hunt. She hurts a small animal. Then, she brings it to her cubs. She gives them the chance to chase and kill it. The cubs play games. The games help them run fast. They play tag, and they wrestle. The cubs will be good hunters in about three years.

After the cubs grow up, the females leave. They go off on their own. They have their own cubs. Brother cheetahs might stay together for life. They work as a team to hunt. They pick a **territory**. That is where they hunt. They protect the land together.

pad: thick cushion on the bottom of an animal's foot
lungs: the organs in the body that allow creatures to breathe; part of the respiratory system
reflect: to throw back light
territory: an area an animal or group of animals lives in and defends

Catch Me if You Can!

Many animals on the African grassland hunt their food. The cheetah seems to know this. Those that do not want to be caught have to run very fast because the cheetah is the fastest land animal on Earth. The cheetah can go from standing still to running 40 miles (64.37 km) per hour in just three steps. In seconds, it can be running 70 miles (112.65 km) per hour.

The cheetah's body helps it to run fast. It has long legs. It has hard **pads** on its paws that help it stop. The cheetah has large **lungs** that help it take deep breaths. It has dark marks under its eyes that look like black tears. They **reflect** the sun's light and keep it from blinding the cheetah. Its bones are lightweight too. It uses its speed to hunt and run away from its enemies.

The cheetah is a good hunter. It has to guard the food it kills. Larger animals might take the meat. If this happens, the cheetah has no food that day. It cannot hunt again until it has rested for a day.

A mother cheetah teaches her babies how to hunt. She hurts a small animal and brings it to her cubs. They chase and kill it. The cubs play games that will help them run fast too. They love to play tag and wrestle.

After the cubs grow up, the females leave. They go off to have cubs of their own. Brother cheetahs often stay together for life. They work as a team to hunt. They pick a **territory** that will be their hunting ground. They protect the land together.

pad: thick cushion on the bottom of an animal's foot
lungs: the organs in the body that allow creatures to breathe; part of the respiratory system
reflect: to throw back light
territory: an area an animal or group of animals lives in and defends

● ● ●

Catch Me if You Can!

Answer the questions.

Read the first paragraph of the passage again.

I. What is the main idea of the first paragraph?

  A. to tell the reader that a cheetah's body helps it run fast
  B. to tell the reader that a cheetah's mother raises it to run fast
  C. to tell the reader that a cheetah is a fast hunter
  D. all of the above

2. Which of the following definitions of *territory* is used in the story?

  A. land where cheetahs raise babies
  B. land where cheetahs hunt
  C. land where cheetahs go to die
  D. land where cheetahs wait to be taken to zoos

3. Which of the following definitions of *run* is used in the story?

  A. to move one's legs with speed, faster than walking
  B. to flow under pressure, as in water
  C. to operate or be in charge of
  D. all of the above

Answer the questions. Write your answers in complete sentences.

4. What does the author say is the reason that cheetah cubs play games?

  _____

  _____

5. What does the author say is the reason that a cheetah has large lungs?

  _____

  _____

6. A cheetah's body is built to help it run fast. On another sheet of paper, write a paragraph explaining how the cheetah's body helps it run fast. Use facts from the story to help you.

The Huge Hunter

The polar bear lives in the coldest place on Earth. Its body keeps it warm. The polar bear has fur all over. Even its feet are furry. You might think a polar bear's fur is white. It is not! A polar bear has clear fur. It looks white because it reflects the sun's light. Each hair is **hollow**. The sun's heat moves through the fur. The polar bear has black skin. Its skin traps the sun's heat. A polar bear also has a thick layer of fat. It may be more than four inches (10.16 cm) thick.

The polar bear hunts on the snow. It has huge claws. This keeps the bear from slipping. The polar bear also hunts in the water. The bear's feet are webbed. This helps it swim. It is a good diver. It can see under the water. The polar bear can be still on the ice. It finds a hole a seal makes in the ice. It can wait near one for hours. The seal will poke its nose up to breathe. Then, the polar bear grabs it. It pulls the seal onto the ice. Polar bears eat a lot of seal meat. But, polar bears are having a hard time hunting.

Polar bears live in the Arctic. The word *arctic* comes from a Greek word. It means "the home of the great bear." Experts say that global warming is changing the polar bear's home. It is changing the bear's habits. The ice in the Arctic is thinner. And, it is **shrinking** in size. What does this mean for the bear? The bear needs the ice to hunt seals. Seals are its main food. Experts are watching the polar bears. They are also watching the warm weather. They want to know if the bears can **survive**.

hollow: nothing inside; not solid
shrinking: becoming smaller in size
survive: to keep existing

The Huge Hunter

The polar bear lives in the coldest place on Earth. Its body keeps it warm. The polar bear has fur all over. Even its feet have fur on them. You might think a polar bear's fur is white. It is not! A polar bear has clear fur. It looks white because it reflects the sun's light. Each hair is **hollow**. The sun's heat moves through the fur. The polar bear has black skin. Because black is the best color to trap the sun's heat, the bear's skin helps keep it warm. A polar bear also has a thick layer of fat.

The polar bear hunts on the snow. It has huge claws. The claws keep the bear from slipping. The polar bear also hunts in the water. It is a good diver. It can see under the water. On the ice, the polar bear can be patient and still. The polar bear looks for an airhole that a seal has made in the ice. It can wait beside one of these holes for hours. When the seal pokes its nose up to breathe, the bear grabs it. It pulls it onto the ice. Seal meat is the main part of the polar bear's diet. But, it is getting harder for polar bears to hunt.

Polar bears live in the Arctic. The word *arctic* comes from a Greek word. It means "the home of the great bear." Experts say that global warming is changing the polar bear's home. It is changing the polar bear's habits. The ice in the Arctic is thinner. And, it is **shrinking** in size. What does this mean for the polar bear? The polar bear needs the ice to hunt seals. Seals are its main food. Experts are watching the bears. They are watching the warm weather. They wonder if the polar bears can **survive**.

hollow: nothing inside; not solid
shrinking: becoming smaller in size
survive: to keep existing

The Huge Hunter

What would you do if you had to hunt in a very cold place? You might dress warmly! The polar bear lives in the coldest place on Earth. Its body keeps it warm. The polar bear has fur all over, even on its feet! You might think a polar bear has white fur. It does not! A polar bear has clear fur that looks white because it reflects the sun's light. Each hair is **hollow** so that the sun's heat can move through it. The polar bear has black skin. Because black is the best color to trap the sun's heat, the bear's skin helps keep it warm. A polar bear also has a thick layer of fat that insulates it.

The polar bear hunts on the snow and in the water. It has huge claws that keep it from slipping. The bear's webbed feet help it swim. It is a good diver, and it can see underwater. On the ice, the polar bear can be patient and still. The polar bear looks for an airhole a seal has made in the ice. The bear can wait there for hours without moving. When the seal pokes its nose up to breathe, the polar bear grabs it and pulls it onto the ice. Seal meat is the main part of the polar bear's diet. But, weather changes are making it harder for bears to hunt.

Polar bears live in the Arctic. The word *arctic* comes from a Greek word that means "the home of the great bear." Experts say that global warming is changing the polar bear's home and its habits. The ice in the Arctic is thinner, and it is **shrinking** in size. What does this mean for the polar bear? The polar bear needs the ice to hunt seals. Experts are watching the bears and the warming weather. They wonder if the polar bears can **survive**.

hollow: nothing inside; not solid
shrinking: becoming smaller in size
survive: to keep existing

The Huge Hunter

Answer the questions.

1. Even the polar bear's _____ have fur on them.

2. The polar bear's _____ is black to hold in the sun's heat.

3. The main thing polar bears eat is _____.

Write **T** for true or **F** for false.

4. _____ The polar bear can swim, but it cannot dive.

5. _____ The polar bear's fur helps to keep it warm.

6. Look at the chain of events. Answer the question.

> A polar bear finds a seal's airhole.
>
> ↓
>
> The polar bear waits near the airhole.
>
> ↓
>
> The polar bear grabs the seal.
>
> ↓
>
> The polar bear pulls the seal onto the ice and eats it.

Which step is missing?

　　A. The polar bear dives into the water.

　　B. The seal comes onto the ice.

　　C. The seal pokes its nose through the airhole to breathe.

　　D. The bear shares the seal meat with its family.

7. What do you think will happen to the polar bears? Write a paragraph on another sheet of paper to explain your answer.

Friend or Foe?

What does a cat do when it traps a mouse? Does it have a meal? Not all of the time! There was a cat named Huan. Huan chased mice all of her life. She ate each one of them. Once, she caught a baby mouse. She did not kill it. She made friends with it!

Huan's owner named the mouse Jerry. The two friends slept in the same bed. They drank from the same bowl. Huan kept other cats away. Jerry helped Huan. He cleaned her paws. How can a cat be friends with a mouse?

This strange **twist** happens sometimes. Experts do not know why. Owners at an Arizona park put this to the test. They chose animals that should not be friends. They chose mountain lions, gray wolves, and black bears. They put them all in one part of the park. They did not know if the animals would hurt each other. They did not think they would. The experts were right! A female wolf took the lead. She went to the mountain lions. She let them sniff her. Soon, these **enemies** were playing. Then, the wolf made friends with the bears. Why did it turn out so well? No one knows.

Sometimes, animals take care of **orphans**. This might happen even when the baby is not the same type as the mother. Once, there was a big storm in Africa. A baby hippo lost its mother. The baby was taken to a park. A giant tortoise became its mother! The mother tortoise cared for it.

---

twist: something unusual or unexpected
enemy: one who seeks to harm or hurt another
orphan: animal or person who has lost parents

Friend or Foe?

What does a cat do when it catches a mouse? It has a meal, right? Not always! Once, there was a cat named Huan. She had chased mice her whole life. She had always eaten them. But, once she caught a baby mouse. She did not kill it. She became friends with it!

People called the mouse Jerry. The two friends played together. They slept in the same bed. They drank milk from the same bowl. Huan kept other cats away from Jerry. Jerry cleaned Huan's paws.

What is going on here? How could a cat and a mouse become friends?

This strange **twist** happens from time to time. No one knows why. Once, the owners of a park in Arizona planned a test. They chose animals that should not be friends. They chose mountain lions, gray wolves, and black bears. They put them together in one part of the park. Would they hurt each other? The owners thought they would not. They were right. A female wolf took the lead. She went to the mountain lions. She let them sniff her. Soon, these **enemies** were playing together. Then, the wolf made friends with the bears. Why did it turn out so well? No one knows.

Sometimes, animals take care of **orphans**. This can even happen when the orphan is not the same kind of animal as the mother! Once, in Africa, there was a storm. A baby hippo lost its mother. The baby was taken to a wildlife park. A giant tortoise became its mother! The tortoise took care of the hippo.

twist: something unusual or unexpected
enemy: one who seeks to harm or hurt another
orphan: animal or person who has lost parents

Friend or Foe?

What happens when a cat catches a mouse? It has a meal, right? Not always! Sometimes in the animal world, things do not turn out as you think they might. Huan had chased mice her whole life. She had always eaten them. But, one day, she caught a baby mouse. She did not kill it. Instead, she became friends with it!

People called the mouse Jerry. The two friends stayed together. They played together. They slept in the same bed. They drank milk from the same bowl. Huan kept other cats away. Jerry cleaned Huan's paws. How could a cat and a mouse become friends?

This strange **twist** in the animal world can happen sometimes. No expert can explain how this sudden trust between animals happens. Once, the owners of a wildlife park in Arizona planned a test. They chose animals that should not be friends. They chose mountain lions, gray wolves, and black bears. They put them together in one part of the park. The owners thought that they would not hurt each other. They were right. A female wolf took the lead. She went to the mountain lions and lay down on the ground. She let the lions sniff her. Soon, these **enemies** were playing together. Then, the wolf made friends with the bears. Why did it turn out so well? No one knows.

Sometimes, animals take care of **orphans**. This can even happen when the orphan is not the same kind of animal as the new mother! Once, in Africa, a baby hippo lost its mother in a big storm. The baby was taken to a wildlife park. It was adopted by a giant tortoise! The tortoise took care of the hippo.

twist: something unusual or unexpected
enemy: one who seeks to harm or hurt another
orphan: animal or person who has lost parents

Friend or Foe?

Answer the questions.

1. _____ was a cat that made friends with a mouse.

2. One of the enemies of the gray wolf is a _____.

3. Read the following sentence from the story and answer the question.

   They chose mountain lions, gray wolves, and black bears.

   Which of the following words would best replace *chose* in this sentence?

   A. found

   B. searched

   C. caged

   D. selected

4. Look at the title of this story. Which of the following has the opposite meaning of *foe*?

   A. enemy

   B. advisor

   C. villain

   D. friend

Circle the number of syllables in each word.

5. expert   one   two

6. female   one   two

7. twist   one   two

8. The author says that scientists cannot explain how a sudden trust happens between animals. On another sheet of paper, write your own ideas about how or why it may happen.

It Is Raining Cats and . . . Frogs?

There was some **strange** weather on September 7, 1953. It happened in Leicester, Massachusetts. It rained frogs and toads! Kids could fill their pails with them! Some thought that the frogs and toads hopped out of a pond. They said the water was too high. But, others said they saw the frogs and toads fall from the sky. They found them on their roofs!

Frog and toad rain might be strange. But, an event in Memphis, Tennessee, may have been stranger. In 1877, it rained black snakes! Some of the snakes were one foot (30.48 cm) long. Some were one and one-half feet (45.72 cm) long. Some people thought the snakes came from a windstorm. But, wind would have picked up other things too. Only snakes fell from the sky. If it was wind, why didn't other things fall?

A rain of animals could come from a big storm. They could be picked up from a sea or lake. Sometimes, water from a pond is sucked up by wind. Then, it rains down somewhere else. Maybe that is what happened in Tiller's Ferry, South Carolina. It rained fish there in 1901. It rained **trout** and catfish. Fish were found in **puddles** in the fields.

Other places have had strange rain too. Rocks, golf balls, ducks, and candy have dropped from the sky! Keep your eyes open for the next storm. You might have strange rain too!

strange: not normal or expected
trout: a common type of fish
puddle: a little bit of water on the ground

It Is Raining Cats and . . . Frogs?

There was some **strange** weather on September 7, 1953. It happened in Leicester, Massachusetts. It rained frogs and toads! Kids could fill their pails with them! Some thought that the frogs and toads hopped out of a pond. They said the water was too high. But, others said they saw the frogs and toads fall from the sky. They found them on their roofs!

Frog and toad rain might be strange. But, an event in Memphis, Tennessee, may have been stranger. In 1877, it rained black snakes! Some of the snakes were one foot (30.48 cm) long. Some were one and one-half feet (45.72 cm) long. Some people thought the snakes came from a windstorm. But, wind would have picked up other things too. Only snakes fell from the sky. If it was wind, why didn't other things fall?

It is easy to see how a rain of animals from the sea or a lake could happen during a big storm. Sometimes, water from a pond is sucked up by huge wind. Then, it rains down somewhere else. Maybe that is what happened in Tiller's Ferry, South Carolina. It rained fish there in 1901. It rained **trout** and catfish. Fish were found in **puddles** in the fields.

Other places have had strange rain too. Rocks, golf balls, ducks, and candy have dropped from the sky! Keep your eyes open for the next interesting storm. It might be in your town!

strange: not normal or expected
trout: a common type of fish
puddle: a little bit of water on the ground

It Is Raining Cats and . . . Frogs?

Have you had any **strange** weather in your town this week? Even if you have, it probably will not top September 7, 1953. That is the day it rained frogs and toads in the town of Leicester, Massachusetts! The streets were covered with leaping frogs. Kids could fill their pails with them! A newspaper writer thought that the frogs and toads hopped out of a pond. They said the water overflowed. But, people said they saw the frogs and toads fall from the sky. They found them on the roofs of their houses!

This "frogfall" was **probably** less scary than what happened in Memphis, Tennessee, in 1877. There, it rained thousands of black snakes! The snakes ranged from one foot (30.48 cm) long to one and one-half feet (45.72 cm) long. Some thought the snakes may have been swept up in a huge windstorm. When the storm ended, the snakes fell from the sky. But, if that were true, why didn't twigs, and other things fall along with the snakes?

It is easy to see how a rain of animals from the sea or a lake could happen during a big storm. Water from a pond is sucked up by huge wind. Then, it rains down somewhere else. That could be what happened in Tiller's Ferry, South Carolina. It rained fish there in 1901. **Trout** and catfish fell in a heavy rain from the sky. Fish were found in **puddles** in the cotton fields.

Other places have had strange rain too. Rocks, golf balls, ducks and candy have dropped from the sky! Watch out! The next interesting storm could be in your town!

strange: not normal or expected
probably: likely, with almost certainty
trout: a common type of fish
puddle: a little bit of water on the ground

1.RI.1, 1.RI.2, 1.RF.2 1.W.3

It Is Raining Cats and . . . Frogs?

Answer the questions.

Write **T** for true and **F** for false.

1. _____ Snakes rained down on the town of Leicester in Massachusetts.

2. _____ Some of the strange weather events have happened after windstorms.

3. _____ Catfish and dogfish rained down on Tiller's Ferry, South Carolina.

4. What is the main idea of this article?

   A. Some towns have had snakes and frogs rain down on them.

   B. Scientists think that windstorms cause strange weather.

   C. Sometimes strange weather happens, and scientists are not sure why.

   D. Animals cause some scary rainstorms.

Read each sentence. Circle to tell whether the underlined word has a long vowel sound or a short vowel sound.

5. The <u>snake</u> is one foot (30.48 cm) long.   long   short

6. <u>Fish</u> rained from the sky.   long   short

7. Kids filled their pails with <u>toads</u>.   long   short

8. Imagine that you are a child standing on the streets of Leicester, Massachusetts, on September 7, 1953. On another sheet of paper, write a short story describing what you see and do. Include facts you read in the story.

Once Upon a Time

When a machine is first made, it is brand new. No one has thought of it. People's lives are changed. But, new ideas do not stay new. Other inventions take their places.

The **abacus** helped people count. It was a board with beads on it. Before the abacus, people used their fingers to count. They kept **track** of the numbers in their heads. Some people were scared of this strange invention. They did not know if they should count so high.

The printing press was brand new too. Before 1450, books were **rare**. They were written by hand. It could take years to make one book. Then, a man named Johannes Gutenberg changed things. He found a way to make type. The type was made out of blocks. Gutenberg carved letters into the blocks. He fitted them into a frame. The machine put ink against paper. In 1452, he made 200 books. Today, we can print lots of books at once. Computers make printing faster.

Today, computers are **extreme** machines. There are people who can recall life before computers. Now, computers are all over. They help cars run. They keep track of our files. They fly planes. They cook food. One day, people will look back. They will think computers seem old. Today, the abacus seems old. The printing press does too. One day, even computers will seem old.

---

abacus: a beaded board used for counting
track: to follow an order of events
rare: not easy to find
extreme: very advanced, passing other ideas

Once Upon a Time

When a machine is first made, it is a breakthrough. No one has ever thought of it. It changes people's lives. But, new ideas do not stay new. Other inventions take their places.

The **abacus** was a counting board with beads on it. It changed everything. Before the abacus, people counted on their fingers. They had to keep **track** of the numbers in their heads. Some people were scared of this strange invention. They did not know if people were meant to count so high.

The printing press was brand new too. Before 1450, books were **rare**. They were written by hand. If you wanted a book, you had to wait a long time. It could take years to make one book. Then, a man named Johannes Gutenberg changed things. He figured out a way to make type. The type was made out of wooden blocks. Gutenberg carved letters into the blocks. Then, he fitted them into a frame. The machine put ink against paper. In 1452, he made 200 books. People were amazed. Today, we can print lots of books at once. Computers make printing faster.

Today, computers are **extreme** machines. There are people who can recall life before computers. Now, computers are all over. They help run cars. They keep track of our files. They fly planes. They cook food. One day, people will look back. They will think computers seem old. Today, the abacus seems old. The printing press does too. One day, even computers will seem old.

abacus: a beaded board used for counting
track: to follow an order of events
rare: not easy to find
extreme: very advanced, passing other ideas

Once Upon a Time

Is every machine on the cutting edge? Maybe! When something is first made, it is a breakthrough. No one has ever thought of it before. It changes the way people live. But, the amazing machines of the past do not stay on the cutting edge. Other inventions take their places.

The **abacus**, a counting board with beads on it, changed everything. Before it was invented, people counted on their fingers. They kept track of the numbers in their heads. Some people were afraid of this strange invention. They did not know if people were meant to count so high.

The printing press was a big breakthrough too. Before 1450, books were **rare**. They were written by hand. If you wanted a book, you had to wait a long time. It could take years to make one book. Then, a man named Johannes Gutenberg changed things. He figured out a way to make type. The type was made out of wooden blocks. Gutenberg carved letters into the blocks and fitted them into a frame. The machine pressed ink against paper. In 1452, he made 200 books. People were amazed. Today, we can print thousands of books at once. Computers help to make text changes and run printing machines.

Computers are the **extreme** machines of our times. There are people who can remember a time before there were computers. Now, computers are everywhere. They are part of our lives. They help run cars. They keep track of our records. They fly planes and cook food. When people look back, they may think our computers seem old-fashioned, like the abacus and the printing press. One day computers will no longer seem extreme.

abacus: a beaded board used for counting
track: to follow an order of events
rare: not easy to find
extreme: very advanced, ahead of other ideas

Once Upon a Time

Answer the questions.

Rewrite each sentence. Use the correct capitalization and punctuation.

1. an abacus was used to help people keep track of high numbers

_____

_____

2. do you think the printing press was an important invention

_____

_____

Write the matching adjective on each line. Use the adjectives in the box.

strange   wooden   long

3. People had to wait a _____ time for a book.

4. People thought the abacus was a _____ invention.

5. The type was made out of _____ blocks.

6. Write the main idea of the last paragraph. Then, list three details that support the main idea. Write your answer in complete sentences.

_____

_____

7. Think about a new machine that may have been invented in your lifetime. Why do you think it is a breakthrough? Write your answer in complete sentences on another sheet of paper.

Quack, Quack!

Ducks can go from land to water. That is true of the bird. It is also true of the trucks and cars called *ducks*. You may have seen a duck in a movie. But, this **transportation** is real.

Ducks were used during World War II. The first ducks were big trucks. They were shaped like tanks. They were huge. They could take troops from a ship to the land. The trucks could carry **supplies** from land onto the water. They were big and slow. But, they helped keep the soldiers safe.

After the war, some people in the United States bought ducks. They were used for tours. In cities like Philadelphia, Pennsylvania, you can ride in a duck. The duck takes you to sights on land. Then, it drives into the water!

These old army trucks are not the only ducks out there. People have invented new ducks. They are fast sports-car ducks. They are more like movie cars. These ducks are small and **sleek**. They move fast on land. Some can drive up to 100 miles per hour (160.93 kmh). Their wheels **flip** up when they are in the water. They become boats! These ducks go between 30 and 40 miles per hour (48.28 and 64.37 kmh) in water. That is a lot faster than the old World War II ducks. Those ducks could go about 6 miles per hour (9.66 kmh) in the water.

It would be fun to own a sports-car duck. But, ducks are useful too. Some people think they could be ambulances. Cities like Seattle, Washington, have a lot of water. A duck ambulance could save lives.

---

transportation: a way to travel from one place to another
supplies: items that are needed for a group to survive
sleek: having a straight and smooth shape
flip: a quick turn or movement

Quack, Quack!

Ducks can go from land to water. That is true of the bird. It is also true of the trucks and cars called *ducks*. You may have seen a duck in a movie. But, this land-to-water **transportation** is real.

Ducks were used during World War II. The first ducks were big, heavy trucks shaped like tanks. The huge trucks could take troops from a ship to the land. The trucks could carry **supplies** from land onto the water. They were big and slow. But, they helped keep the troops safe.

After the war, some people in the United States bought ducks. They were used to give rides. In cities like Philadelphia, Pennsylvania, you can ride in a duck. The duck takes you to sights on land. Then, it drives into the water!

These old army trucks are not the only ducks out there. People have made new ducks. They are fast sports-car ducks. They are more like movie cars. These ducks are small and **sleek**. They move fast on land. Some can drive up to 100 miles per hour (160.93 kmh). To go in the water, the wheels **flip** under the cars. They become boats! These ducks go between 30 and 40 miles per hour (48.28 and 64.37 kmh) in water. That is a lot faster than the old World War II ducks. Those ducks could only travel about 6 miles per hour (9.66 kmh) in the water.

It would be fun to own a sports-car duck. But, ducks are useful too. Some people think ducks could be ambulances. Cities like Seattle, Washington, have a lot of water and islands. A duck ambulance could save lives.

transportation: a way to travel from one place to another
supplies: items that are needed for a group to survive
sleek: having a straight and smooth shape
flip: a quick turn or movement

Quack, Quack!

Ducks can go from land to water. That is true of the bird. It is also true of the trucks and cars called *ducks*. You may have seen a duck in a spy movie. But, this land-to-water **transportation** is real.

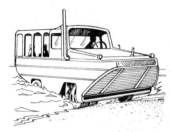

Ducks were used during World War II. The first ducks were big, heavy trucks shaped like tanks. The huge trucks could take troops and **supplies** from a ship to the land. The trucks could drive from land onto the water. They were big and slow, but they helped keep soldiers safe.

After the war, they were used for tourist rides. In cities like Philadelphia, Pennsylvania, you can ride in a duck. The duck takes you to sights on land, and then it drives into the water!

These old army trucks are not the only ducks out there. People have invented new ducks—fast sports-car ducks. They are more like spy-movie cars. These ducks are small and **sleek**. They can move very fast on land, up to 100 miles per hour (160.93 kmh). In order to go in the water, the cars must go down a slope or a beach. Once a duck is in the water, the wheels **flip** under the car. It becomes a boat! In the water, these cool cars can go between 30 and 40 miles per hour (48.28 and 64.37 kmh). That is a lot faster than the old World War II ducks, which can only travel about 6 miles per hour (9.66 kmh) in the water.

Just having a sports-car duck for fun is not its only possible use. Some people are working to make the new ducks into ambulances. In cities like Seattle, Washington, where there is a lot of water and many islands, an ambulance that could speed from land to water could save lives.

transportation: a way to travel from one place to another
supplies: items that are needed for a group to survive
sleek: having a straight and smooth shape
flip: a quick turn or movement

Name _____

Quack, Quack!

Answer the questions.

Match each word to the word that has the opposite meaning.

1. _____ fast   **A.** tiny

2. _____ huge   **B.** boring

3. _____ exciting   **C.** slow

4. Read the following sentence from the story and answer the question.

   These ducks are small and sleek.

   Which word means almost the same as *sleek*?

   A. clunky

   B. dull

   C. streamlined

   D. silly

5. Write a question about the sports-car duck. Write an answer to your question. Write your answer as a complete sentence.

   _____

   _____

Circle the correct word or phrase to complete each sentence.

6. A duck (is, is not) a submarine that can go on land.

7. The sports-car duck's (brakes, wheels) flip under the car in the water.

8. People want to use a sports-car duck as an ambulance or a water taxi. What other good uses can you think of for a sports-car duck? On another sheet of paper, explain your ideas for ways people could use a sports-car duck. When you have finished, read it to a classmate. Ask your classmate for suggestions. Then, revise your paragraph.

Frozen Delight

One night in 1905, an 11-year-old boy was mixing fruit drinks. His name was Frank Epperson. Frank put soda powder in the drinks. Frank lived in California. He knew that it would be cold that night. He wondered how his drink would taste if it froze. He put the glass outside. He left his wooden stirring stick in the glass.

In the morning, Frank looked at the glass. The drink was frozen solid! In the center was his wooden stick. Frank slid the treat out of the glass. He held it by the stick. It was good! He called it "the Ep-sicle."

Frank did not have the money to make and sell his treat. But, there was one more **problem**. In 1905, people did not have freezers in their homes. How would they keep the Ep-sicles frozen?

Over the years, Frank **invented** more things. But, no one wanted to make and sell Frank's **products**. Frank knew he was on his own. He would have to make his products himself. He thought of all of his products. Which would be the cheapest to make and sell? Then, he thought of the Ep-sicle.

Frank made a machine. It was a mold for his snacks. He also made a machine that would stamp his name on the sticks. Frank's son George thought of a good name. George called Frank "Pop." Guess what George called the treat?

Frank made his treats by himself for two years. He sold seven flavors. In 1925, a company bought Frank's idea. Today, people eat millions of Frank's sweet treats. It all started with an 11-year-old boy!

problem: a difficulty; something that is hard to deal with
invent: to produce something useful for the first time
product: something that is made or grown to be sold

Frozen Delight

One night in 1905, an 11-year-old boy was mixing fruit drinks. His name was Frank Epperson. Frank added soda powder to the drinks. Frank lived in California. The weather report said that it would be cold that night. He wondered how his drink would taste if it was frozen. He put the glass outside. He left his wooden stirring stick in the glass.

In the morning, Frank looked at the glass. The drink was frozen solid! In the center was his wooden stick. Frank slid the treat out of the glass and held it by the stick. It was good! He called it "the Ep-sicle."

Frank did not have the money to make and sell his treat. But, there was one more **problem**. In 1905, people did not have freezers in their homes. How would they keep the Ep-sicles frozen?

Many years passed. Frank kept **inventing** things. Nobody wanted to make Frank's products. He would have to make his products himself. He thought of all of his **products**. Which would be the **cheapest** to make? Then, he thought of the Ep-sicle.

Frank made a machine that molded his snacks. He also made a machine to stamp his name on the sticks. Frank's son, George, thought of a better name. He called Frank "Pop." Guess what George called the treat?

Frank made his treats by himself for two years. He sold seven flavors. In 1925, a company bought Frank's idea. Today, people eat millions of Frank's sweet treats. It all started with an 11-year-old boy!

problem: a difficulty; something that is hard to deal with
invent: to produce something useful for the first time
product: something that is made or grown to be sold
cheap: a low price

Frozen Delight

One night in 1905, an 11-year-old boy was mixing fruit drinks. His name was Frank Epperson. Frank lived in California. The weather report said that it would be cold that night. He wondered how his drink would taste if it was frozen. He put the glass outside. He left his wooden stirring stick in the glass.

The next morning, Frank went outside to get his glass. The fruit drink was frozen solid. Standing in the center was his wooden stick. Frank slid the treat out of the glass by the stick. It tasted good! He called it "the Ep-sicle."

Frank did not have the money to make or sell his sweet treat. But, there was one more **problem**. In 1905, people did not have freezers in their homes. How would they keep the Ep-sicles frozen?

Many years passed. Frank kept **inventing** things. Sadly, nobody wanted to make and sell Frank's products. He would have to make his **products** himself. He thought of all of his products. Which would be the cheapest to make and sell? He thought of the Ep-sicle.

Frank made a machine that molded the ice-cold snacks. He also made a machine that would stamp his name on the sticks. But, Frank's son George thought of a better name. George called Frank "Pop." Guess what George called the treat?

In 1925, a company paid Frank so that it could make and sell his frozen treat. something he had invented! Since then, this cool idea by an 11-year-old boy has become big business. People eat millions of Frank's sweet "icicles" every year.

problem: a difficulty; something that is hard to deal with
invent: to produce something useful for the first time
product: something that is made or grown to be sold

Frozen Delight

Answer the questions.

1. Frank Epperson invented a frozen treat when he was _____ years old.

2. The first name Frank gave his treat was _____.

3. The year Frank invented his treat was _____.

Write each date correctly.

4. november 3 1905 _____

5. june 9 1912 _____

6. What name do you think George Epperson gave his father's frozen treat? _____

7. Look at the chain of events below and answer the question.

> Frank invents a new treat when he is 11 years old.

> ↓

> Frank invents many other things, but none of them sell.

> ↓

> Frank invents a machine to mold the treats.

> ↓

> A company buys Frank's idea so that it can make the treats.

Which step is missing?

    A. Frank decides to stop inventing things.
    B. Frank decides that if he wants to sell one of his inventions, he must make it himself.
    C. Frank gives the idea for the treats to his son George.
    D. Frank gives up on the Ep-sicles and makes a new kind of cereal.

8. Read the following sentence and answer the question.

Frank did not think of a very good name for his treat.

Do you agree or disagree? Why? Write your answer on another sheet of paper.

Talk to the Animals

Dylan Scott Pierce loved to draw. He started when he was two years old. He drew lions. He drew dinosaurs. Lots of kids like to draw. But, Dylan was not the same. His pictures looked **lifelike**. Dylan won an art prize when he was nine years old. When he was 10, people were buying his work. Some of his paintings sold for $20,000!

Dylan was schooled at home. This gave him time for his art. Dylan has a hobby too. He takes photos. He uses them when he plans a painting.

Dylan's work is sold all over the world. He likes to use watercolor. This is a thin paint. It helps him make light. It also lets him make shadows. He has also used pencils and oil paints.

Most of the time, Dylan paints animals. Dylan has a pet cat. But, he loves all kinds of animals. Dylan makes lots of trips to zoos. People at zoos know him. They let him get close to the animals. He watches them. He takes photos. Once, he even swam with sea animals!

In 2003, Dylan went on a **safari**. He saw all kinds of animals in their **habitats**. Baboons jumped on his roof. He saw a herd of giraffes. An elephant chased them! Dylan painted a picture. It was an elephant. It showed how proud and free the animal was in its home. Dylan could not have done the painting after watching animals in a zoo.

Dylan liked his trip. He went to Africa again. This time, he saw lions. Dylan had painted lions for years. But, this was not the same. One lion looked him right in the eyes! This trip was more than five weeks long. Dylan now gives money to Africa. He wants to help the animals and people there.

lifelike: looking like a real person or thing
safari: a journey to see animals, especially in Africa
habitat: the type of place where a plant or animal usually grows or lives

Talk to the Animals

Dylan Scott Pierce was two years old when he started to draw. He loved to draw lions and dinosaurs. Lots of kids like to draw. But, Dylan was not the same. His pictures looked **lifelike**. Dylan won an art prize when he was nine years old. When he was 10, people bought his work. Some of his paintings sold for $20,000!

Dylan was schooled at home. This gave him time for his art. He also takes photos. He uses them when he plans a painting.

Dylan's paintings are sold all over. He likes to use watercolor. This thin paint helps him make light. It also lets him make shadows. He has also used pencils and oil paints.

Most of the time, Dylan paints animals. Dylan has a pet cat. But, he loves all kinds of animals. Dylan makes many trips to zoos. He is well known at zoos. People let him get close to the animals. He watches them and takes photos. Once, he even swam with sea animals!

Dylan had not seen animals in their **habitats**. He went to Africa in 2003. Dylan went on **safari**. Dylan saw all kinds of animals. Baboons jumped on his roof. He saw a herd of giraffes. An elephant chased them! Dylan painted a picture of it. It showed how proud and free the animal was in its own home. Dylan could not have done the painting after going to a zoo.

Dylan liked his trip. He went to Africa again. This time, he saw lions. Dylan had painted lions for years. This was not the same. One lion looked him right in the eyes! This trip was more than five weeks long. Dylan uses some of the money he makes to help the people and animals of Africa.

lifelike: looking like a real person or thing
habitat: the type of place where a plant or animal usually grows or lives
safari: a journey to see animals, especially in Africa

Talk to the Animals

Dylan Scott Pierce was two years old when he started to draw. He loved to draw lions and dinosaurs. Lots of young children like drawing. Dylan's drawings were different. They were **lifelike**. When Dylan was only nine years old, he won first place in an art contest. By the time Dylan was 10, people lined up to buy his work. Some of his paintings have sold for $20,000!

Dylan was schooled at home. This gave him time for his artwork. He also takes photos. Sometimes, he uses his photos when he plans a painting.

Dylan's paintings are sold all over the world. He likes to use watercolor. It helps to create light and shadows when he paints. He has also used pencils and oil paints.

Most of the time, Dylan paints animals. He loves all kinds of animals. Dylan makes many trips to zoos. He is well known at zoos. People let him get close to the animals. He watches and takes photos of them.

Dylan had not seen animals in their **habitats**. In 2003, Dylan went on a **safari** in Africa. Baboons jumped on his roof. He saw a herd of giraffes. An elephant chased them! Dylan painted a picture of it. It showed how proud and free the animal was in its own home. Dylan could not have done the painting after going to a zoo.

Dylan went to Africa again. The second time, he saw lions. Dylan had painted lions for years. This was different. One lion looked him right in the eyes! He stayed in Africa for more than five weeks. He uses some of the money he makes to help the people and wild animals of Africa.

lifelike: looking like a real person or thing
habitat: the type of place where a plant or animal usually grows or lives
safari: a journey to see animals, especially in Africa

 © Carson-Dellosa · CD-104613 · Differentiated Reading for Comprehension

Talk to the Animals

Answer the questions.

Read the sentence. Answer the question.

1. List three types of animals that are mentioned in the story.

_____

2. Why does the author say that Dylan could not have painted his picture of an elephant after going to a zoo?

    A. Zoos do not have elephants.

    B. Dylan could not find a zoo with an elephant he wanted to paint.

    C. An elephant in a zoo would not look as free and proud as the one in his painting.

    D. He never thought about painting elephants until he went to Africa.

3. How old was Dylan when he first started drawing?

    A. two years old   **B.** nine years old

    C. 10 years old   **D.** 12 years old

Circle the correct verb in each sentence.

4. Dylan (draw, draws) lions and elephants.

5. The lions (walk, walks) proudly through the trees.

6. Other kids (paint, paints) with watercolor too.

7. The safari driver (show, shows) us how to make a fire.

8. Imagine that you are on safari in Africa. What do you see? What do you hear? On another sheet of paper, write a short story telling about your adventure. Be sure your story has a beginning, a middle, and an end.

Be Amazing!

Kids do some **amazing** things. You can too! Kids all over the world do amazing things.

Each person has a **talent**. The things you like to do are clues. You can learn to be good at things. Start with the things you like to do.

Do you love to paint? Do you like to draw? You could take art lessons. Go to an art show. Talk to the artists. Take a pad of paper with you any place you go. Draw the things you see.

Maybe you love math. There might be an older child who could teach you about math. You could help **tutor** younger kids. You can learn a lot from being a student. You can learn a lot from teaching someone else!

Would you like to work with animals? Help out at an animal shelter. You could talk to a vet. Maybe you could visit a farm. You could learn from the farmer.

Do you want to make movies? You can make a home movie. Start with a storyboard. This is a plan of pictures the camera will shoot. Ask your friends to play the parts. Then, get started.

Maybe you want to help people. There are lots of things kids can do. They can start a drive to collect clothes for the homeless. They can collect food for food banks. Find a way to help. Start today!

So, do not be afraid. Find your gift. Look inside yourself. Be proud. You can do amazing things. All you have to do is learn, try, and do!

amaze: to fill with wonder or surprise
talent: the ability to do something especially well
tutor: a private teacher teaching one student

Be Amazing!

Kids do some **amazing** things, and you can too! Kids all over the world do amazing things.

Everyone has a **talent**. The things you like to do are clues. You can learn to be good at things. Start with the things you like to do.

Do you love to paint? Do you like to draw? You could take art lessons. Go to an art show. Talk to the artists. Take a pad of paper with you any place you go. Draw the things you see.

Maybe you love math. There might be an older child who could teach you about math. You could help **tutor** younger kids. You can learn a lot from being a student, and you can learn a lot from teaching someone else!

Would you like to work with animals? Help out at an animal shelter. You could talk to a vet. Maybe you could visit a farm, and you could learn from the farmer.

Do you want to make movies? You can make a home movie. Start with a storyboard. That is a plan of pictures the camera will shoot. Ask your friends and family to play the parts. Then, get started.

Maybe you want to help people. There are lots of things kids can do. They can collect clothes for the homeless. They can collect food for food banks. Find a way to help. Start today!

So, do not be afraid. Find your gift. Look inside yourself. Be proud. You can do amazing things. All you have to do is learn, try, and do!

amaze: to fill with wonder or surprise
talent: the ability to do something especially well
tutor: a private teacher teaching one student

Be Amazing!

Kids do some **amazing** things, and you can too! Kids all over the world do amazing things every day.

First, choose what you really want to do. Everyone has a **talent**. The things you like to do are clues. You can learn to be good at things, but start with the things you like to do.

Do you love painting or drawing? Go to an art show and talk to the artists. Take a pad of paper with you wherever you go and draw pictures of what you see.

Maybe you love numbers. There might be an older child who could teach you about math. You could help **tutor** younger children. You can learn a lot from being a student, and you can learn a lot from teaching others!

Would you like to work with animals? Help out at an animal shelter. You could talk to a vet. Visit a farm and learn about the farm animals.

Do you want to make movies? You can make a home video. Start with a storyboard, a plan of pictures the camera will shoot. Ask your friends and family to play the parts. Then, get started.

Maybe you want to help people. Kids can start a drive to collect clothes for the homeless, and they can collect food for food banks.

So, do not be afraid. Look inside yourself and be confident. You can do amazing things. All you have to do is learn, try, and do!

amaze: to fill with wonder or surprise
talent: the ability to do something especially well
tutor: a private teacher teaching one student

Be Amazing!

Answer the questions below.

Circle the correct pronoun in each sentence.

1. The artist told us about his paintings. (He, Him) teaches art lessons.

2. The boys borrowed a video camera. (He, They) are going to make a movie.

3. Julie is writing a story. (She, Her) will read it to us later.

Answer each question. Use the word box on the story page to help you.

4. What is a *talent*?

   A. a special skill

   B. a bird's claw

   C. a piece of rope

   D. a kind of story

5. What is a *tutor*?

   A. a type of piano

   B. a drawing contest

   C. a math problem about shapes

   D. a teacher who helps one student

6. Why does the author say that every kid can be amazing?

   A. Kids do amazing things every day.

   B. All kids have special things they love to do.

   C. Kids will do best if they choose to do what they like best.

   D. all of the above

7. What talent do you have that you would like to learn more about? How could you learn more? On another sheet of paper, write your answer in complete sentences.

Warrior Queen

The army fought for 10 years. It won the **kingdom** piece by piece. The head of the army was a woman. She wore armor. She rode a white horse. She was a **warrior**. She was a queen. Her name was Isabella of Castile.

In the 1400s, women did not lead battles. Isabella was not a normal woman. She was not a normal queen. She ruled a piece of land. Her husband ruled another piece of land. They ruled with the same power. They went to war together. They took over another piece of land. Today, the three kingdoms are Spain.

Isabella was brave. She liked things her own way. She set up schools. She made a big library. Her son was schooled. Her daughters were schooled too.

We remember Isabella for one choice she made. She helped Christopher Columbus. He wanted to sail across the sea. He thought he would find a new path to the Indies. Isabella helped him pay for his ships and supplies. He found the New World. He came back a year later. He brought gold and **Native** Americans. Isabella ruled that the native people must be treated well.

No woman during her time had the same kind of power. Isabella fought hard to unite Spain. She was not scared to rule. She was not scared to lead in a world led by men.

kingdom: a country ruled by a king or queen
warrior: a person who fights in a battle, known for courage and skill
native: from a particular place by birth

Warrior Queen

For 10 years, the army fought. It won the **kingdom** piece by piece. The head of the army was a woman. She wore armor and rode a white horse. She was a **warrior** and a queen. Her name was Isabella of Castile.

In the 1400s, women did not lead battles. Isabella was not a normal woman. She was not a normal queen. She ruled a piece of land. Her husband ruled another piece of land. They ruled with the same power. They went to war and took over a third piece of land. Today, the three kingdoms are Spain.

Isabella was brave. She liked things her own way. She set up schools. She made a big library of books and writings. Her son was schooled. But, she made sure her daughters were schooled too.

We remember Isabella for one choice she made. She helped Christopher Columbus. He wanted to sail across the sea. He thought he would find a new path to the Indies. Isabella helped him pay for his ships and supplies. He came back from the New World a year later. He brought gold and **Native** Americans. Isabella ruled that the native people must be treated well. She even wrote this in her will.

No woman during her time had the same kind of power. Isabella fought to unite Spain. She was not scared to rule. She was not scared to lead in a world led by men.

kingdom: a country ruled by a king or queen
warrior: a person who fights in a battle, known for courage and skill
native: from a particular place by birth

Warrior Queen

For 10 years, the army fought. It won the **kingdom** piece by piece. The head of the army was a woman. She wore armor and rode a white horse. She was a **warrior** and a queen. Her name was Isabella of Castile.

In the 1400s, women did not lead battles. Isabella was not a normal woman. She was not a normal queen. She ruled a piece of land. Her husband ruled another piece of land. They ruled with the same power. They went to war together and took over a third piece of land. Today, the three kingdoms are Spain.

Isabella was brave. She made sure she had things her own way. She set up schools. She put together a big library of books and writings. She had her daughters schooled along with her son. One of her daughters married King Henry VIII. She became Queen of England.

Today, we remember Isabella for one choice she made. She chose to help an explorer named Christopher Columbus. He wanted to sail west across the ocean. He was looking for a new path to the Indies. Isabella helped him pay for his ships and supplies. One year later, he returned from the New World. He brought gold and **Native** Americans. Isabella declared that the native people must be treated well. She even wrote this in her will so that it would be clear after her death.

No woman during her time had the same kind of power. Isabella fought hard to unite Spain. She was not scared to be a ruler. She was not scared to be a leader in a world led by men.

---

kingdom: a country ruled by a king or queen
warrior: a person who fights in a battle, known for courage and skill
native: from a particular place by birth

Warrior Queen

Answer the questions below.

1. Circle three adjectives that describe Isabella.

quiet	bold	meek
weak	brave	determined

2. Circle three adjectives that describe an ocean.

little	blue	wet
dry	soft	huge

Write the correct word in each blank. Use one of these words.

but   so   because

3. Long ago, women did not ride into battle, _____ Queen Isabella was not like other women.

4. We remember Queen Isabella _____ she was not scared to be a great leader.

5. Christopher Columbus needed money, _____ he asked the queen for help.

6. The author says that Queen Isabella was brave. Do you think Christopher Columbus was brave too? Why or why not?

_____

_____

_____

_____

7. Queen Isabella was a great leader. On another sheet of paper, write a short paragraph about someone else who is a great leader. Give reasons to support your choice.

Exploring the Arctic

Explorers in the Arctic take a lot of risks. Lots of explorers tried to get to the North Pole first. More than 800 explorers died trying to get there.

An explorer named Robert Peary thought his team could make it. He felt good because Matthew Henson was with them. Henson was an **experienced** guide and explorer. He worked for Peary. Henson had spent years learning about the Arctic. He knew the language of the **Inuit**. He knew how to build igloos. He knew how to hunt for food in the snow. He knew how to drive a dogsled team.

Something stopped Peary and Henson on each of their trips. One time, they almost starved to death. Another time, the ice melted before they could get there. Peary lost eight toes to frostbite. It seemed that they would never get to the North Pole.

In 1908, Peary said his team would try one more time. He asked Henson to go with the team. Peary was sure they could not make it without Henson. So, Matthew Henson prepared for one more trip to the Arctic.

Henson took great care to plan their trip. This time, they left food in igloos along the way. They would eat this food on the way back. Henson was the best dogsled driver on the team. He led the way. He made a trail for the rest.

On April 6, 1909, Matthew Henson stopped his sled. He did not need to go any farther. He was at the top of the world. Henson, Peary, and their crew were at the North Pole. They were the first people to **triumph** over this world of ice and snow.

experienced: having knowledge from taking part in an event or activity in the past
Inuit: the native people of the Arctic
triumph: have victory

Exploring the Arctic

The Arctic is filled with danger. Many people wanted to be the first to stand at the North Pole. More than 800 explorers died trying to get there.

An explorer named Robert Peary thought his team could make it. He felt good because Matthew Henson was with them. Henson was an **experienced** guide and explorer. He worked for Peary. Henson had spent years learning about the Arctic. He knew the language of the **Inuit**. He knew how to build igloos and hunt for food in the snow. He knew how to drive a dogsled team.

Something stopped Peary and Henson on each of their trips. One time, they almost starved to death. Another time, the ice melted before they could get there. Peary lost eight toes to frostbite. It seemed that they would never get to the North Pole.

In 1908, Peary said his team would try one more time. He insisted that Henson go with the team. Peary was sure they could not make it without Henson. So, Matthew Henson prepared for another trip to the frozen Arctic.

Henson took great care to plan their trip. This time, they left food in igloos along the way. They would eat this food on the way back. Henson was the best dogsled driver on the team. He led the way. He made a trail for the rest.

On April 6, 1909, Matthew Henson stopped his sled. He did not need to go any farther. He was at the top of the world. Henson, Peary, and their crew were at the North Pole. They were the first people to **triumph** over this world of ice and snow.

experienced: having knowledge from taking part in an event or activity in the past
Inuit: the native people of the Arctic
triumph: have victory

Exploring the Arctic

The Arctic is filled with danger. Many people wanted to be the first to stand at the North Pole. By the beginning of the 1900s, more than 800 explorers had died trying to get there.

An explorer named Robert Peary was sure that his team could make it. He might not have been so sure if he had not had the help of Matthew Henson. Henson was an **experienced** guide and explorer. He worked for Peary. Henson had spent years learning about this cold, frozen world. He knew the language of the **Inuit**. He knew how to build igloos. He knew how to hunt for food in the snow and ice, and how to drive a dogsled team.

Each time Peary and Henson tried to reach the North Pole, something stopped them. One time, they almost starved to death. Another time, the ice had melted. It seemed that they would never succeed.

In 1908, Peary said his team would try one more time. He insisted that Henson go with the team. Peary was sure they could not make it without Henson. So, Matthew Henson prepared for another trip to the frozen Arctic.

Henson planned their trip carefully. They left stores of food in igloos along the way. They would eat this food on the way back. Henson was the best dogsled driver on the team. So, he took the lead and made a trail for the rest.

On April 6, 1909, Matthew Henson stopped and waited for the other sleds to catch up. Henson, Peary, and their crew were at the North Pole. They were the first people to **triumph** over this world of ice and snow.

---

experienced: having knowledge from taking part in an event or activity in the past
Inuit: the native people of the Arctic
triumph: have victory

Exploring the Arctic

Answer the questions below.

1. Who are the *Inuit*?

    A. They are the people who live in the Arctic.

    B. They are people who build igloos.

    C. They are people who know how to hunt in the ice and snow.

    D. all of the above

Write **T** for true and **F** for false.

2. _____ Matthew Henson worked for an explorer named George Peary.

3. _____ The team had plenty of food on every trip.

4. _____ Matthew Henson was the best dogsled driver on the team.

Circle the number of syllables in each word.

5. frozen   one   two

6. Pole   one   two

7. dogsled   one   two

8. Imagine that you are Matthew Henson. If you were planning a trip to the Arctic, what would you take along? Write a paragraph on another sheet of paper. Read the passage again. Use the ideas in the story to help you.

Digging for Dinosaurs

Do you think of Canada when you think of dinosaurs? You should! Dinosaur Provincial Park in Alberta, Canada, is a great place to find dinosaur bones. It is found in a large valley. The valley was made at the end of the last ice age. The melting ice cut into the ground. It made a rock-filled river. Now, the park is in Canada's **badlands**. Badlands are formed by **erosion**.

The badlands do not look like they used to. It was not the same more than 75 million years ago. Then, the area was warm. It had a lot of water. The ground was swampy. It was a great place for dinosaurs to find food. Scientists know this. They have found lots of dinosaur bones there. Scientists have found at least 150 whole dinosaur skeletons! They have also found big piles of dinosaur bones. These are called bone beds.

One bone bed has only one type of bones in it. They are Centrosaurus bones. These huge dinosaurs lived in herds. Scientists think a lot of members of a herd drowned there. Today, scientists are still finding bones there.

Those who go to the park can visit a **museum**. They can see some skeletons. They can also see real places where scientists have looked for bones. People can see digs that are still in progress.

Scientists have found the bones of many types of dinosaurs in the park. They have found 38 different types. The ground was once wet. That kept the bones in good shape. Scientists have also found leaves from plants. These plants grew in the past. The fossils in Canada's Dinosaur Provincial Park can teach us about the past.

> **badlands:** an area with high cliffs, little water, and rocky grounds
> **erosion:** the slow destruction of something by natural forces, such as wind, water, or ice
> **museum:** a building where interesting and valuable things are collected and shown

Digging for Dinosaurs

When you think about dinosaurs, do you think about Canada? You should! One of the best places to find dinosaur bones is in the province of Alberta, Canada. It is the Dinosaur Provincial Park, and it is found in a large valley. The valley was made at the end of the last ice age. The melting ice cut into the ground. It made a rock-filled river. Now, the park is in Canada's **badlands**. Badlands are formed by **erosion**.

The badlands do not look the same way they used to. Then, the area was warm. It had a lot of water. The ground was swampy. It was a great place for dinosaurs to find food. Scientists know this because they have found so many dinosaur bones there. Scientists have found at least 150 whole dinosaur skeletons! They have also found big piles of dinosaur bones. These are called bone beds.

There is one bone bed that has only Centrosaurus bones in it. These huge dinosaurs lived in herds. Scientists think a lot of members of a herd drowned there. Today, scientists are still finding many bones there.

Those who go to the dinosaur park can visit a **museum**. They can see some of the skeletons. They can also see real places where scientists have looked for bones. People can see digs that are still in progress.

Scientists have found the bones of at least 38 different types of dinosaurs in the park. The ground was once wet. That kept bones in good shape. Scientists have also found leaves from plants that once grew. The fossils in Canada's Dinosaur Provincial Park can teach us about the past.

> **badlands:** an area with high cliffs, little water, and rocky grounds
> **erosion:** the slow destruction of something by natural forces, such as wind, water, or ice
> **museum:** a building where interesting and valuable things are collected and shown

Digging for Dinosaurs

When you think about dinosaurs, do you think about Canada? You should! One of the best places to find dinosaur bones is in the province of Alberta, Canada. It is the Dinosaur Provincial Park, and it is found in a large valley. The valley was made at the end of the last ice age. The melting ice cut into the ground. It made a rock-filled river. Now, the park is in Canada's **badlands**. Badlands are formed by **erosion**.

More than 75 million years ago, the badlands looked very different. Then, the area was warm. It had a lot of water. The ground was swampy. It was a great place for dinosaurs to find food. Scientists have found at least 150 whole dinosaur skeletons there! They have also found big piles of dinosaur bones. These are called bone beds.

There is one bone bed that has only Centrosaurus bones in it. These huge elephant-like dinosaurs lived in herds. Scientists think that many members of a herd drowned when they tried to cross a flooded river. All of their bodies sank into the riverbed. Scientists find hundreds of bones there.

Tourists who go to the dinosaur park can visit a **museum** to see some of the skeletons. They can also see actual places where scientists have looked for bones. People can take tours to see digs that are still in progress.

Scientists have found the bones of at least 38 different types of dinosaurs. The ground was once wet, so the bones are in good shape. Leaves from different types of plants have also been found. With these fossils in Canada's Dinosaur Provincial Park, we can learn about the past.

badlands: an area with high cliffs, little water, and rocky grounds
erosion: the slow destruction of something by natural forces, such as wind, water, or ice
museum: a building where interesting and valuable things, such as artwork or historical pieces, are collected and shown

1.RI.1, 1.W.1, 1.L.5

Digging for Dinosaurs

Answer the questions.

Match each word to the word with the opposite meaning.

I. _____ huge   **A.** smooth

2. _____ rocky   **B.** tiny

3. _____ wet   **C.** dry

4. The Centrosaurus was

     A. a type of fossil

     B. a huge dinosaur

     C. a snake-like dinosaur

     D. a type of scientific process

5. What types of fossils have been found at the dinosaur park?

     A. dinosaur bones and small fish

     B. rocks and trees

     C. dinosaur bones and plant leaves

     D. dinosaurs and snails

6. A bone bed is _____

_____

7. The valley of the dinosaur park was made by _____

_____

8. Would you like to help dig for dinosaur bones? Why or why not? On another sheet of paper, write your answer in complete sentences.

The Amazing Amazon

The Amazon River is in South America. It is great and strong. **Freshwater** flows into the Earth's oceans. Some of it comes from this river. There is one river that is longer than the Amazon. It is the Nile River. But, the Amazon is wider and stronger.

The Amazon has a lot of **curves**. Its source is high in the mountains. Its water flows more than 4,000 miles (6,437.38 km) to get to the sea. The **mouth** of the Amazon is more than 150 miles (241.4 km) wide.

Explorers found the river's mouth in 1500. Their ship was 200 miles (321.87 km) away from land. They were on the ocean. But, the group was on freshwater! This was water from the Amazon River.

People have not changed the Amazon much. There is a rain forest around it. Very few people live there. The rain forest trees are being cut down. But, there is not one bridge across the Amazon River.

Lots of **unique** creatures live in the Amazon River. Many large fish live in the Amazon River. Mammals live there too. A type of river dolphin lives there. Catfish there can weigh up to 200 pounds (90.72 kg)! Piranha live in the river too. These scary fish have sharp teeth.

An anaconda is a type of snake. It lives in the rain forest. It is one of the biggest snakes in the world. It floats just under the top of the water.

Thousands of rare creatures live in the rain forest. They each help make the Amazon River the awesome place that it is.

freshwater: water that is not salty
curves: rounded paths
mouth: the place on a river where the water reaches the sea
unique: one of a kind; unusual

The Amazing Amazon

The Amazon River in South America is a mighty force. **Freshwater** flows into the Earth's oceans. About 20 percent of it comes from this river. There is one river that is longer than the Amazon. It is the Nile River in Africa.

The Amazon has a lot of **curves**. Its source is high in the Andes Mountains. Its water flows more than 4,000 miles (6,437.38 km) to get to the sea. The **mouth** of the Amazon is more than 150 miles (241.4 km) wide.

In fact, explorers found the mouth of the Amazon River in 1500. Their ship was 200 miles (321.87 km) away from land. They were on the Atlantic Ocean. But, the group found that their boats were on freshwater coming from the mouth of the Amazon River!

People have not changed the Amazon much. There is a rain forest around it. Very few people live there. The rain forest trees are being cut down. But, there is not one bridge across the Amazon River.

Lots of **unique** creatures live in the Amazon River. A type of freshwater river dolphin lives there. Catfish there can weigh up to 200 pounds (90.72 kg)! Piranha live in the river too. These scary fish have sharp teeth.

An anaconda is a type of snake. It lives in the rain forest. It is one of the biggest snakes in the world. It floats just under the top of the water.

Thousands of rare creatures live in the rain forest. They each help make the Amazon River the awesome place that it is.

freshwater: water that is not salty
curves: rounded paths
mouth: the place on a river where the water reaches the sea
unique: one of a kind; unusual

The Amazing Amazon

The Amazon River in South America is a mighty force. **Freshwater** flows into the Earth's oceans. About 20 percent of it comes from this river. There is one river that is longer than the Amazon. It is the Nile River in Africa.

The Amazon has a lot of **curves**. Its source is high in the Andes Mountains. Its water flows more than 4,000 miles (6,437.38 km) to get to the sea. The **mouth** of the Amazon is more than 150 miles (241.4 km) wide.

Explorers discovered the mouth of the Amazon River in 1500. Their ship was 200 miles (321.87 km) away from land. They were on the Atlantic Ocean. But, the sailors found their boat was on freshwater coming from the mouth of the Amazon River.

The Amazon has not been changed much by people. There is a rain forest around it. Few people live there. There is not one bridge across it.

Many large fish and water mammals live in the Amazon River. A type of freshwater river dolphin, called a boto or pink river dolphin, lives in this wide river. Catfish that live there can grow to weigh 200 pounds (90.72 kg)! Piranha live in the river too. These scary fish have sharp teeth.

An anaconda is a type of snake. It lives in the rain forest. It is one of the biggest snakes in the world. It floats just under the top of the water.

These animals share the river with thousands of rare animals from the rain forest. They each help make the Amazon River the amazing place that it is.

---

freshwater: water that is not salty
curves: rounded paths
mouth: the place on a river where the water reaches the sea

Name _____

The Amazing Amazon

Answer the questions below.

I. Which of the following does not live in the Amazon River?

    A. catfish

    B. anaconda

    C. blue whale

    D. piranha

Circle the correct noun in each sentence.

2. The (sailors, sailor's) hat is red and white.

3. The (ships, ship's) are sailing across the sea.

4. The (dolphins, dolphin's) fin is gliding above the wave.

5. The Brazil nut (trees, tree's) leaves filled the sky and blocked the sun.

Use each word in a sentence. Use the word box on the story page to help you.

            freshwater   mouth

6. _____

_____

7. _____

_____

8. Would you want to go boating on the Amazon River? Why or why not? Write your answer on another sheet of paper. Write your answer in complete sentences.

A National Treasure

Yellowstone National Park is in the western United States. There are rivers, hot pools, and geysers there. The Yellowstone volcano is there. A huge **crater** is there. It was left by the last volcano **eruption**. Earth's **crust** is very thin there. It is thinner than it is in other places.

There are lots of geysers in the park. The world's largest geyser is there. It is named Steamboat. Old Faithful is the most famous geyser there. It erupts about every 90 minutes. Some other geysers are named Plume, Beehive, Castle, and Daisy.

There are many pools in the park. One pool is called Morning Glory. It used to be warm and clear blue. But, tourists have **harmed** it. They threw coins and rocks into the pool. Now it is turning green.

There are many wild animals in the park. The prairie dogs used to be wild. Now, they wait for people to feed them. They beg for treats! This has led to some problems. People think that bears are tame too. They are not.

There are other sights to see in Yellowstone. There are mountains, valleys, a canyon, and a huge lake. Yellowstone Lake is the largest mountain lake in the United States. The Grand Canyon of Yellowstone is a large, rocky canyon with a 308-foot (93.88 m) waterfall on one end. Herds of elk, packs of wolves, and families of moose roam through the valleys.

The features of Yellowstone make it special. In 1872, it was chosen to be the first national park. It offers many natural wonders.

---

crater: large, round hole in the ground
eruption: a sudden explosion that sends out rocks, lava, and ash or hot water and steam
crust: the outer part of a planet
harmed: caused damage to

A National Treasure

Yellowstone National Park is in the western United States. There are rivers, hot pools, and geysers there. The Yellowstone volcano is there. A huge **crater** is there. It was left by the last volcano **eruption**. Earth's **crust** is very thin there. It is thinner than it is in other places.

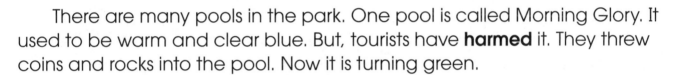

There are lots of geysers in the park. No other place has more geysers. The world's largest geyser is there. It is named Steamboat. Old Faithful is the most famous geyser there. It erupts about every 90 minutes. Some other geysers are named Plume, Beehive, Castle, and Daisy.

There are many pools in the park. One pool is called Morning Glory. It used to be warm and clear blue. But, tourists have **harmed** it. They threw coins and rocks into the pool. Now it is turning green.

There are many wild animals in the park. The prairie dogs used to be wild. Now, they wait for people to feed them. They beg for treats! This has led to some problems. People think that bears are tame too. They are not.

There are other sights to see in Yellowstone. There are mountains, valleys, a canyon, and a huge lake. Yellowstone Lake is the largest mountain lake in the United States. The Grand Canyon of Yellowstone is a large, rocky canyon with a 308-foot (93.88 m) waterfall on one end. Herds of elk, packs of wolves, and families of moose roam through the valleys.

In 1872, Yellowstone was chosen to be the first national park. It offers many natural wonders that cannot be seen anywhere else in the world.

crater: large, round hole in the ground
eruption: a sudden explosion that sends out rocks, lava, and ash or hot water and steam
crust: the outer part of a planet
harmed: caused damage to

A National Treasure

Yellowstone National Park is in the western United States. The Yellowstone volcano is there. A huge **crater** is there. It was left by the last volcano **eruption**. Earth's **crust** is much thinner in Yellowstone than in other places. That is why there are more than 10,000 hot water features that the volcano created in the park, including hot springs and geysers.

The world's largest geyser is in Yellowstone. It is named Steamboat. Old Faithful is the most famous geyser there. Some other geysers are named Plume, Beehive, and Daisy.

There are many pools in the park. One pool is called Morning Glory. It used to be warm and clear blue. But, park tourists have **harmed** it. They threw coins and rocks into the pool. Now it is turning green.

There are many wild animals in the park. The prairie dogs used to be wild. Now, they wait for people to feed them. They beg for treats! This has led to some problems.

There are mountains, valleys, a canyon, and a huge lake in the park. The Grand Canyon of Yellowstone is a large, rocky canyon with a 308-foot (93.88 m) waterfall on one end. There are valleys throughout the park where visitors can see herds of elk, packs of wolves, and families of moose.

The creations of the Yellowstone volcano make the park truly unique. Maybe that is why it was chosen in 1872 to be the first national park in the United States. Yellowstone is a grand place with many natural wonders.

crater: large, round hole in the ground
eruption: a sudden explosion that sends out rocks, lava, and ash or hot water and steam
crust: the outer part of a planet
harmed: caused damage to

A National Treasure

Answer the questions.

1. What did the Morning Glory pool look like before people harmed it?

    A. It had yellow sides and was very deep.
    B. It held warm, blue water.
    C. It was filled with rocks and fish.
    D. none of the above

2. Which of the following is not mentioned in the story?

    A. Yellowstone's animals   **B.** Yellowstone's plants
    C. Yellowstone's water features   **D.** Yellowstone's volcano

3. Why do you think it is unsafe to tame the animals in the park?

    A. They learn to trust people too much and might get hit by a car.
    B. They depend on people for their food instead of finding it for themselves.
    C. Even a tamed animal might bite a person if it is scared.
    D. all of the above

In each row, circle the word that is not spelled correctly.

4. lak   tame   park

5. some   ther   warm

6. pak   most   much

7. If you could name a geyser, what would you name it? Explain your choice.

_____

_____

8. If you were a park ranger at Yellowstone, would you rather work with the animals or at the geysers? Why? Write your answer on another sheet of paper.

Answer Key

Page 7

I. B; 2. D; 3. Crocodiles; 4. leaves; 5. watched; 6. walked; 7. hunts; 8. Answers will vary.

Page 11

I. A; 2. B; 3. A; 4. Cubs play games to help them run fast. 5. Cheetahs have large lungs to help them take deep breaths so that they can run fast. 6. Answers will vary.

Page 15

I. feet; 2. skin; 3. seals; 4. F; 5. T; 6. C; 7. Answers will vary.

Page 19

I. Huan; 2. black bear or mountain lion; 3. D; 4. D; 5. two; 6. two; 7. one; 8. Answers will vary.

Page 23

I. F; 2. T; 3. F; 4. C; 5. long; 6. short; 7. long; 8. Answers will vary.

Page 27

I. An abacus was used to help people keep track of high numbers. 2. Do you think the printing press was an important invention? 3. long; 4. strange; 5. wooden; 6. Answers will vary. 7. Answers will vary.

Page 31

I. C; 2. A; 3. B; 4. C; 5. Answers will vary. 6. is not; 7. wheels; 8. Answers will vary.

Page 35

I. 11; 2. the Ep-sicle; 3. 1905; 4. November 3, 1905; 5. June 9, 1912; 6. popsicle; 7. B; 8. Answers will vary.

Page 39

I. Answers may include cat, sea animals, baboons, giraffes, elephants, lions, and dinosaurs; 2. C; 3. A; 4. draws; 5. walk; 6. paint; 7. shows; 8. Answers will vary.

Page 43

I. He; 2. They; 3. She; 4. A; 5. D; 6. D; 7. Answers will vary.

Page 47

I. bold, brave, determined; 2. blue, wet, huge; 3. but; 4. because; 5. so; 6. Answers will vary. 7. Answers will vary.

Page 51

I. D; 2. F; 3. F; 4. T; 5. two; 6. one; 7. two; 8. Answers will vary.

Page 55

I. B; 2. A; 3. C; 4. B; 5. C; 6. A bone bed is big piles of dinosaur bones. 7. The valley of the dinosaur park was made by melting ice and erosion. 8. Answers will vary.

Page 59

I C; 2. sailor's; 3. ships; 4. dolphin's; 5. tree's; 6. Answers will vary. 7. Answers will vary. 8. Answers will vary.

Page 63

I. B; 2. B; 3. D; 4. lak; 5. ther; 6. pak; 7. Answers will vary. 8. Answers will vary.

Notes

_____

_____

_____

_____

_____

_____